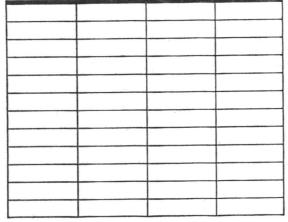

W9-ASL-392

DATE DUE

296.6
WOO
Cy

Wood, Angela
Jewish synagogue

Morrill Math-Science Academy
Chicago Public Schools
6011 S. Rockwell St.
Chicago, IL 60629

Jewish
Synagogue

For Adam Lowenthal

For a free color catalog describing Gareth Stevens' list of high-quality books and multimedia programs, call 1-800-542-2595 (USA) or 1-800-461-9120 (Canada). Gareth Stevens Publishing's Fax: (414) 225-0377.

Gareth Stevens Publishing thanks Reverend Francis Barry Silberg, Ph.D. D.D., for his assistance with the accuracy of the text. Rabbi Silberg is the President and Chairman of Fellows of the Center for the Study of Religion in Milwaukee, Wisconsin. He is also Professor of Theology at Marquette University, in Milwaukee, and the Marcus Scholar-in-Residence in Ethics at the University of Wisconsin-Milwaukee.

Library of Congress Cataloging-in-Publication Data available upon request from publisher.
Fax: (414) 225-0377 for the attention of the Publishing Records Department.

ISBN 0-8368-2608-6

This North American edition first published in 2000 by
Gareth Stevens Publishing
1555 North RiverCenter Drive, Suite 201
Milwaukee, WI 53212 USA

Original edition © 1998 by Franklin Watts.
First published in 1998 by Franklin Watts,
96 Leonard Street, London EC2A 4RH, England.
This U. S. edition © 2000 by Gareth Stevens, Inc.
Additional end matter © 2000 by Gareth Stevens, Inc.

Editor: Samantha Armstrong
Series Designer: Kirstie Billingham
Illustrator: Gemini Patel
Religious Education Consultant: Margaret Barratt, Religious Education Teacher Advisor
Religious Consultant: Laurie Rosenberg, Board of Deputies of British Jews
Reading Consultant: Prue Goodwin, Language and Information Centre, Reading

Gareth Stevens Series Editor: Dorothy L. Gibbs

Photographic acknowledgements:
Cover: Steve Shott Photography; Ann and Bury Peerless.
Inside: p. 6 Fabrizio Bensch/Impact; p. 7 Bruno Barbey/Magnum; p. 24 Ann and Bury Peerless;
p. 25 (top) Carlos Reyes-Manzo, Andes Press Agency, (bottom left) The Hutchison Library.
All other photographs by Steve Shott Photography.

With thanks to The West London Synagogue and United Synagogue, Hendon.

Printed in the United States of America

1 2 3 4 5 6 7 8 9 04 03 02 01 00

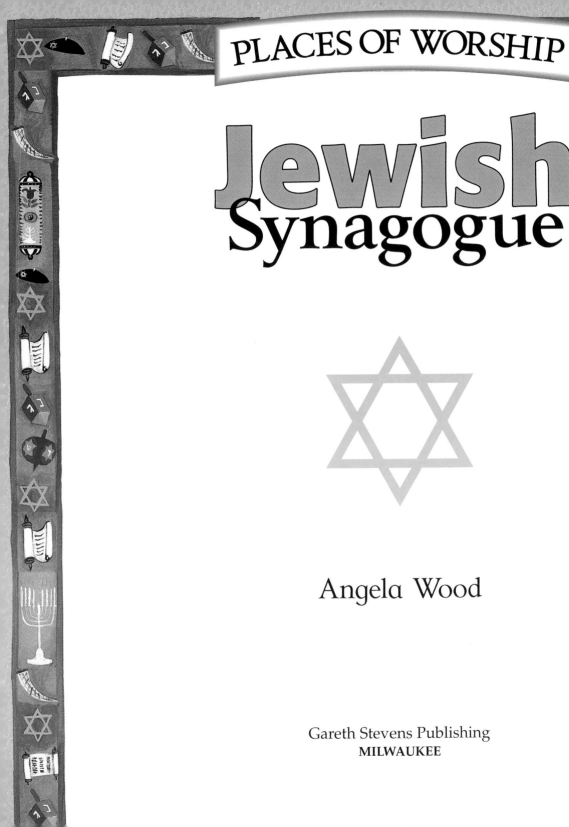

PLACES OF WORSHIP

Jewish
Synagogue

Angela Wood

Gareth Stevens Publishing
MILWAUKEE

The Magen David, or Star of David,
is the symbol sometimes used
to represent the Jewish faith.

Contents

Words that appear in the glossary are printed in **boldface**
type the first time they occur in the text.

A **synagogue** is a place where Jews meet to **worship** God and to study. Some synagogues are small and simple. Others are large and have a lot of decorations. There are synagogues all around the world.

◁ This synagogue is in Germany.

Jewish Beliefs

Jews believe in one God. The special day each week for Jews is called **Shabbat**. It lasts from Friday evening until Saturday night. Many Jews go to the synagogue on Shabbat.

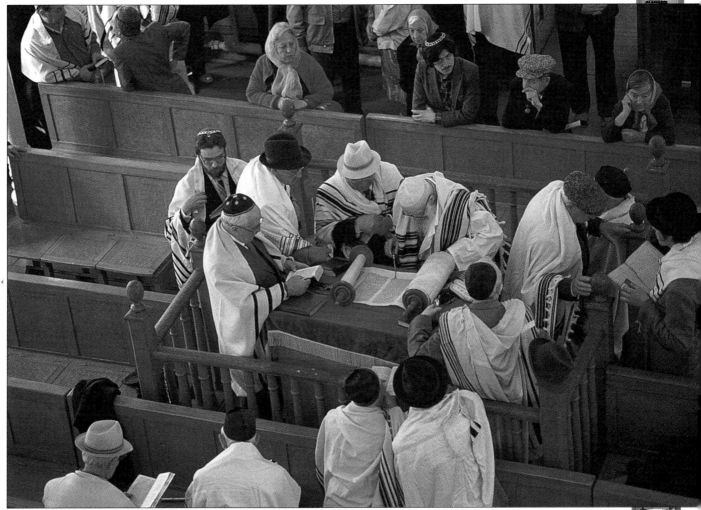

Inside a Synagogue

Every synagogue has a large chamber called an **Ark**. The **Torah scrolls** are kept inside the Ark. The Torah is the special book for Jews. Scrolls are long pieces of rolled-up **parchment**.

◁ When people face the Ark, they are facing in the direction of Jerusalem. Jerusalem is an important city for Jewish people.

Each synagogue also has a platform, called a **bimah**. The person leading the prayers stands on the bimah. In most synagogues, men lead the prayers, but, in some synagogues, women may also lead them.

◁ A teenage boy and girl are on the bimah together. They are reading the Torah.

IN·MEMORY·OF·DAVID·QUIXANO·HENRIQUES·1804-1870·

The Ark

The Ark is a special chamber in which the Torah scrolls are kept. The Torah is a five-book collection of Jewish laws, stories, and teachings about God. Each scroll has a book of the Torah written on it.

On Shabbat and during ▷ Jewish festivals, one of the Torah scrolls is taken out of the Ark to be read. The Torah guides Jewish people in their daily lives.

10

The Eternal Light

Above the Ark is the **Eternal Light**, or **Ner Tamid**. It reminds Jews that the Torah is always there and that God lives forever. It can be an oil lamp or an electric light, but it is always kept lit.

The curtains on the ▷ Ark are closed. The Ner Tamid shines above the Ark.

A Torah Scroll

A Torah scroll is written by hand, and it is written in **Hebrew**. Hebrew is the Jewish language that has been used since ancient times. A **yad** is used to point to the words on the scroll. The scroll is attached to a wooden roller. Sometimes a rolled-up scroll is put inside a cloth cover.

◁ A scroll has a decorative silver breastplate, called a **hoshen**, over the cloth cover.

The silver bells on top ▷ of a scroll are called **rimonim**. When the scroll is carried from the Ark to the bimah, the bells jingle.

A Torah scroll must be undressed before it is read. First, the silver bells are taken off. Then, the yad, the breastplate, and, finally, the cloth cover are removed.

14

Next, the **binder** that keeps the scroll rolled up is untied.

Then, the scroll is unrolled a little bit and is held up high. The person holding the scroll turns in four directions so everyone can see the Torah.

15

Reading from the Torah

Before and after the Torah is read, one person sings a blessing to thank God for the Torah. The people in the synagogue join in for part of the blessing. While the Torah is being read, everyone follows along carefully to make sure the words are read exactly as they are written down.

◁ When people read from a Torah scroll, they point to the words with a yad. *Yad* is the Hebrew word for "hand."

Getting Ready for Prayer

For morning prayers, all men and older boys wear a shawl called a **tallit**. In some synagogues, women and older girls also wear a tallit when they pray. A tallit usually has blue or black stripes and fringe along the edges.

On each corner of the tallit, long, thin pieces of fringe, called **tzitzit**, are knotted in a special way. Tzitzit reminds Jews about God and the Torah.

◁ The tallit is often kept in a cloth bag. The Hebrew lettering on this bag spells "tallit."

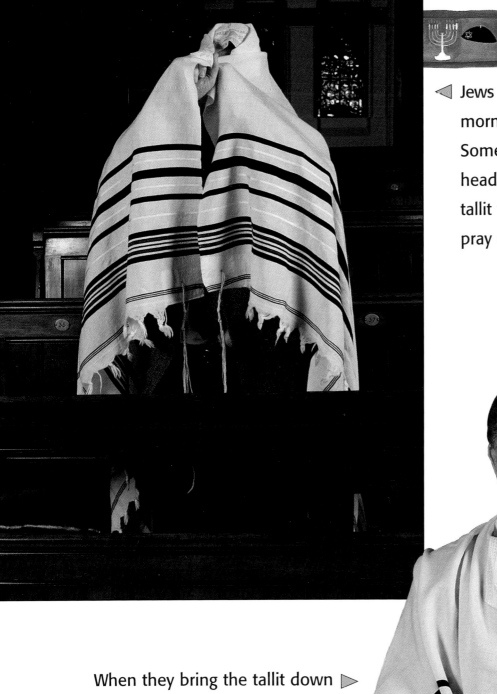

Jews put on a tallit before morning prayers begin. Some Jews cover their head and face with the tallit for a moment and pray or think in private.

When they bring the tallit down ▷ onto their shoulders, they are ready for morning prayers.

A synagogue holds three **services** a day. Jews can pray alone, but they usually pray together. Most of the prayers say *we*, *us*, and *our*.

Any adult Jew can lead the prayers. Sometimes a **rabbi** leads them. A rabbi is a teacher and a preacher.

Jews usually pray in Hebrew, but, in some synagogues, some prayers are in the ordinary language of the people.

Ten Commandments

The **Ten Commandments** are the most important part of the Torah. When they are read from a scroll, everybody stands up. Most of the commandments are rules.

Here is a simple version of the Ten Commandments:

1. *I am God. I love you, and I give you freedom and hope.*

2. *Only pray to God.*

3. *Use God's name only at special times.*

4. *Every week, celebrate a day of rest, peace, and happiness.*

5. *Care about your parents.*

6. *Love life and living things.*

7. *Protect your family.*

8. *Do not steal.*

9. *Be honest.*

10. *Do not get jealous.*

The first words of the Ten ▷ Commandments appear in Hebrew on the wall of this synagogue. They are written on the shapes of two stone slabs because that is how they were first written down.

אנכי ה׳
לא יהיה
לא תשא
זכור את
כבד את
לא תרצח
לא תנאף
לא תגנב
לא תענה
לא תחמד

Jewish Art

There are no pictures of God or statues in the synagogue. Jews believe that God does not have a body. They also believe it is wrong to worship people. Most Jewish art is about the Torah, the land of Israel, and the first Jewish temple of long ago.

◁ This candlestick has seven branches, like a tree. It is called a menorah. There was a menorah in the ancient temple in Jerusalem.

24

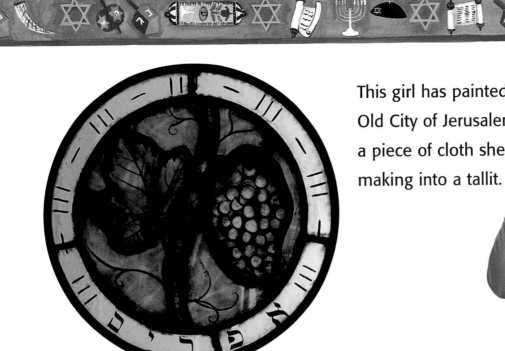

The vine in this picture stands for the land of Israel and the Jewish people because the branches of a vine weave around each other.

This girl has painted the ▷ Old City of Jerusalem on a piece of cloth she is making into a tallit.

This symbol is called ▷ a Magen David, or Star of David. There were twelve tribes in Israel, and the star has twelve edges.

25

Synagogue Activities

Most synagogues have classes for children after school or on Sunday mornings. In these classes, children learn about the Torah, Jewish history and festivals, and how to read Hebrew. There are classes for adults and families, too.

◁ These children are making pictures with sand to celebrate the Jewish festival of Hanukkah.

On a day before ▷ Hanukkah, these children are learning how to make olive oil and light the menorah.

Glossary

Ark: the special chamber where the Torah scrolls are kept.

bimah (bee-mah): the platform in a synagogue where a person stands to lead the prayers and to read the Torah scrolls.

binder: a sash that is tied around a Torah scroll to keep it from unwinding.

Eternal Light: a light above the Ark that shines all the time.

Hebrew: the ancient language of the Jewish people, still used today for prayers and readings.

hoshen (hoh-shen): a silver breastplate that is placed over the cloth cover of a Torah scroll.

Ner Tamid (Nair Tah-meed): the Hebrew word for the light that shines above the Ark.

parchment: a kind of paper that is thick but not stiff and was originally made from animal skin.

rabbi (rab-eye): a Jewish teacher and preacher.

rimonim (ree-moan-eem): the silver bells attached at the top of the roller on a Torah scroll.

scrolls: long pieces of rolled-up parchment with writing on them.

services: meetings in a synagogue at which Jews pray and read the Torah together.

Shabbat (Shah-<u>baht</u>): the special day each week, lasting from Friday evening until Saturday night, when many Jews take part in religious services.

synagogue: a building where Jews meet to pray and study.

tallit (tahl-<u>eet</u>): a shawl worn by all Jewish men and some women for morning prayers.

Ten Commandments: an important part of Torah law that tells Jews how to live their daily lives.

Torah (Toe-<u>rah</u>): a five-book collection of Jewish laws, stories, and teachings.

tzitzit (zeet-zeet): the fringe that is knotted together in a special way on one of the four corners of a tallit.

worship: to show love and respect with prayer, usually as part of a religious service.

yad (yahd): the hand-shaped pointer used to follow the words in the Torah.

More Books to Read

The Always Prayer Shawl.
  Sheldon Oberman
  (Boyds Mills Press)

The Book of Miracles:
  A Young Person's Guide
  to Jewish Spiritual
  Awareness. Lawrence
  Kushner (Jewish Lights)

I Am Jewish. Religions
  of the World (series).
  Bernard P. Weiss
  (Rosen/Powerkids Press)

Inside the Synagogue.
  Joan G. Sugarman and
  Grace R. Freeman
  (Union of American
  Hebrew Congregation)

Israel. Festivals of the
  World (series). Don Foy
  (Gareth Stevens)

Judaism. World Religions
  (series). Angela Wood
  (Thomson Learning)

Kids Explore America's
  Jewish Heritage. Kids
  Explore (series). Westridge
  Young Writers' Workshop
  (John Muir Publications)

The Menorah Story.
  Mark H. Podwal
  (Greenwillow)

Starlight and Candles:
  The Joys of the Sabbath.
  Fran Manushkin
  (Simon and Schuster)

What Do We Know
  About Judaism? What
  Do We Know About...?
  (series). Doreen Fine
  (Peter Bedrick Books)

Videos

The Gates of Jerusalem.
(Questar)

Israel.
(Clearvue/eav. Inc.)

Jewish-American Heritage. American Cultures for Children (series). (Schlessinger Media)

Web Sites

Family Shabbat Table Talk
uahc.org/shabbat

Jewish Funland
www.bus.ualberta.ca/ yreshef/funland/ funland.html

Judaism 101
www.jewfaq.org/

Torah Tots
www.torahtots.com/ index.htm

Your Jewish Connections for Children.
www.geocities.com/ EnchantedForest/Dell/ 4430/jewish.htm

To find additional web sites, use a reliable search engine with one or more of the following keywords: *Hanukkah, Hebrew, Israel, Judaism, menorah, religion, Shabbat, synagogue, Talmud,* and *Torah.*

Index